REINSURANCE FOR BEGINNERS

Mohammed Sadullah Khan

DEDICATION

Dedicated to my family members for their patience and understanding.

Increasing Complexities of Business has increased the scope
of Reinsurance

REINSURANCE FOR BEGINNERS

- Financial Stability
- Geographical Spread of Risk
- Solvency Margins and other Financial Features
- Providing Catastrophic Protection
- Risk Management and Underwriting Expertise

- Proportional Reinsurance
- Non-Proportional Reinsurance
- Facultative Reinsurance
- Treaty Reinsurance
- Quota Share Treaty
- Surplus Treaty
- Excess of Loss
- Stop Loss Cover

1. <u>Introduction</u>

The evolution of current state of humanity along with the vast developments in the Science and Technology has given rise to many concepts which were unknown few centuries earlier or may be even few decades earlier. Initially there were small business even barter system, later on we have seen the growing complexities of businesses, we have seen small ships, buildings, industries and transportation, then their sizes and complexities increased tremendously.

The Airline Industry developed very fast and now we find huge Aero-planes, so is the case of Sea transport and Land transport. The launching of satellites into the orbits has increased and is expected to rise. The complexities and sizes of business, the accumulation of risks and losses due to catastrophes like Tsunami, Floods and Earthquakes has increased tremendously. Future may give rise to more complex and huge exposures.

Reinsurance is the terminology with which most of insurers are familiar but general public may not be so well aware of. If we look at it plainly it is similar to insurance which an ordinary layman purchases. The only difference is that Reinsurance is available to the Insurance Companies and not to the ordinary customers. In insurance the insured is the person who needs protection and he buys protection by way of the insurance. Whereas the Insurance companies who deal in different kinds of risks also need to protect themselves hence they have to buy insurance to protect them-selves.

Reinsurance is very vital to the insurance industry. The globalization and the internet revolution has made the Reinsurance transactions much easier and helped the reinsurers in mapping their risks in-order to avoid accumulations. Almost all of the Insurance Markets in the world are regulated. This has resulted in increasing compliances with the regulators and their requirements.

A majority of Insurance Companies would like to retain the small to medium risks which are good and profitable. In case of huge risks, in-order to protect portfolios certain restrictions are imposed by the Regulators. The Insurers are left with no option but to reinsure their risks with local or International Insurers. Even otherwise as a good practice and protection against huge losses it is always recommended to have a proper Reinsurance in place.

As already mentioned professional Reinsurance Companies deal with Insurance Companies and they make it a point not to deal with direct public. However there are Insurance Companies who are registered to transact both Insurance and Reinsurance. They accept direct business from the Market and reinsurance business from other Insurance Companies. Internally they may have their own separation of the both kind of businesses.

Insurance Companies are concerned about their capacities. Reinsurance gives them a chance to underwrite the risks which are beyond their capacity.

Our definition of Reinsurance is "the transfer of the complete or partial risk by the Insurance Company to the Reinsurer". The process of Re-insurance can be done directly by the Insurance Company or through one of the brokers known as Reinsurance broker.

The intention of this book is provide a simple and easy understanding of Re-Insurance.

2. <u>History of Reinsurance</u>

As we know that Insurance evolved during late 16th century. During that period Marine Insurance volume was rising rapidly and this gave rise to the concept of Reinsurance to protect the interests of the Insurers. It was visible directly in year 1746 and it was related to the Marine business. In fire the first treaty seems to be signed in the year 1821.

After Industrial revolution, the Insurance and Reinsurance business developed rapidly. We have seen two world wars and after which there was a rapid development in the technology and production methods.

Gradually the Lloyd's also started writing Reinsurance

business. In the current scenario we find that Reinsurance forms a huge portion of their business. It is well known fact that one can deal with Lloyds through a Lloyds Brokers only.

The first form of Reinsurance was a facultative type. Later on various models were developed depending upon the demand and requirements of the Market. Nowadays we find a variety of Insurance Contracts.

Insurance is the business where huge money is collected from the Insured, saved and invested to be paid at the time of misfortune or after an agreed period of time. To protect the Insured and Society from the misuse and abuse of the custodians of their funds almost all the Governments in the world have regulated their Insurance Industry. These regulations gradually became applicable to the Reinsurers and their contracts also.

During last few decades we have also seen the development of Computers, Science and technology which transformed the World into Global village. The Catastrophic losses like Terrorist attack on twin towers in USA, Hurricane, Tsunami, Icelandic Volcanic eruptions have further strengthened the importance and workings of Re-Insurance.

3. <u>Legal aspects of Reinsurance – Principles of Insurance</u>

Insurance in simple terms is nothing but the "losses of few shared by many". The same principle is involved in the concept of Re-insurance. In-order to understand the Reinsurance principles we should understand the basic Principles of Insurance. In Reinsurance usually one Insurer (better known as Reinsurer) will normally takes the risk from the Insurer (the Insurance Company) and it writes the contract and promises to indemnify them in case of loss. The agreement is accepted and agreed upon by the Insurance Company and the Reinsurance Company. The company purchasing the reinsurance is known as the Primary or the Ceding Insurer, the company selling the reinsurance is known as the Reinsurance Company or the Reinsurer.

holds good and true. Not providing the correct information may jeopardize the whole contract. In-case of doubt as to whether to provide the information to the Insurer, it is better to provide the information.

Duty of Utmost good faith is applicable to all the parties to the Insurance Contract. The Insurance company should also provide the information related to its products its terms and conditions. A customer may be able to take a knowledgeable decision if he has the right information. Hence it is required on part of the insurer to provide the right and detailed information to the insured.

For individual most of the insurance companies insist upon submission of proposal forms which contain sufficient information related to Utmost Good Faith. Some forms also contain information as to what need to be disclosed before and during the currency period of the contract.

In Reinsurance the principle of Utmost good faith plays a major and important role. If we look nowadays we find almost all Insurance companies have automatic treaties with their Reinsurers. The Reinsurers rely on the information provided by the Insurance Companies and they follow the fortunes of the Insurance Companies. Both the parties should have an honest and trust worthy dealings as far their contract goes. The Reinsurance contracts are the contracts of "Uberrimae Fidei", which is a Latin phrase for Utmost good faith.

Another term used for Reinsurance is "insurance of insurance companies". Re-insurers are taking the risks of the insurance companies and any losses incurred by the Insurance Company, is transferred on to the Reinsurer by way of Reinsurance Contract or agreement. The Reinsurer by virtue of their huge capacity and global reach are able to spread the risks throughout the world.

Usually Reinsurers are cautious risk takers and they want the Insurance Companies to retain some of the risks. This makes them feel more comfortable. If the Insurance Company has a stake in the risk then they will be more responsible and will not take risks which may cause them harm. The amount of risk retained by the Insurance Companies is known as retention.

Even Reinsurance Companies want to protect themselves from dangerous levels of risks hence in-order to protect themselves against losses they buy Insurance to protect them-selves, which is known as Retrocession. The Insurance Company, rather we can say the Reinsurance Company which is providing the coverage is known as Retro-cessionaire. Some time's the Reinsurance Companies share the Risk among themselves, which is known as Co-Reinsurance.

The Insurance Company which is passing its Risk to the Reinsurance Company is known as Primary Insurer. The Insurance contract is between the Insurance Company/Primary Insurer and the Reinsurance Company.

The insured may not even be aware of the Re-insurance contract. In case of default of payment by the Reinsurer, the Primary Insurer is liable to pay the losses (provided the same is covered by the policy) to the insured. The insured may not be in a position to approach the Reinsurance Company in case of default by the Insurance Company. The moment the Primary Insurer accepts the risk it creates an insurable interest in the risk, by virtue of which it can place the risk with the Reinsurer.

As the insurance evolved few centuries earlier, with its evolution the principles guiding the Insurance also evolved. Justice cannot be done to any topic on insurance without the understanding of these principles. These principles are also applicable to the concept of Reinsurance. We will try to understand the six principles of Insurance, which are as follows,

a) Utmost Good Faith
b) Insurance Interest
c) Indemnity
d) Subrogation
e) Contribution
f) Proximate Cause

a) <u>Utmost Good Faith</u>

Let us understand each one of the above principles. The First and the foremost principle of Insurance is known as the Principle of Utmost Good Faith.

In product marketing we abide by the principle of Good Faith. Suppose you are buying a Refrigerator you go to the showroom and buy the product by paying the price quoted by the Salesman and you are not disclosing any information related to you or your activities. Even the Salesman is not supposed to disclose any information unless asked for and if any information is asked by the client then he is supposed to provide the right information. It is guided by the principle of "let the buyer beware" or in Latin it is called as "Caveat Emptor".

If you are hiring a taxi, you ask the driver to take him to a particular location and he will quote his price without him interested in knowing anything about you. You are also not asking about his information and his antecedents. Once he drops you to the place agreed upon you will pay the amount agreed upon.

But Insurance contracts are over and above this. They are termed as contracts of Utmost Good Faith. Utmost Good faith is nothing but it is duty of disclosure. What needs to be disclosed is the question, which comes to our mind. We need to disclose all the information which helps the insurers in taking decision whether to insure us or to reject our proposal. If he is accepting the proposal then the information helps him in providing the terms and conditions to the policy. Hence it is very essential that all the information should be provided to the Insurers.

There is a saying that we should provide the right information to the Doctors, Lawyers and Insurers. Thi

b) Insurance Interest

The second most important principle of Insurance is Insurance Interest. A person without insurable interest cannot buy insurance policy.

If we want to understand from a laymen's perspective Insurable Interest is simply Ownership. You have insurable interest if you own the item or subject matter to be insured. But on a broader front without ownership if you have financial interest then it is considered as an insurable interest. The entity who is staking a claim under the policy should be the person suffering the financial loss. This gives wider scope to the understanding of the principle of Insurable Interest. The Garages, which are handling the vehicles belonging to the customers, can cover the vehicles of the customer in-spite of them being not the owners of the vehicle. An individual or group, who has financially interest in another person, can also create insurable interest.

The policy issued by the Insurance Company should be as per the terms of agreement between the Cedant and the Reinsurance Company. In Reinsurance also if the Insurance Company has Liability then only the Reinsurer's Liability arises.

The other principles such as Principle of Indemnity, Contribution, Subrogation, Proximate Cause are either directly or indirectly applied under Reinsurance Contracts. We will try to understand these principles in detail.

c) Indemnity

All forms of Reinsurance are treated as contracts of Indemnity. "Indemnity" is the third most important principle of Insurance and comes into play when there is a claim. The principle of Indemnity states that the person suffering the financial loss should be compensated equal to the loss he suffered. He should be in the same financial position after the loss as he was before the loss.

Suppose a Car meets with an accident and if one of its door is damaged and the cost of replacement of the door with labor charges is US $ 3,000. Then he should be paid US $ 3,000. But in practice this may not happen as policies have conditions like deductible or excess and depreciation condition. However the spirit of the principle should be followed in the practice of Insurance. The insured should not be better off nor worse off from the accident.

On the other hand if there is a deductible of US$ 500 then the claims will be settled for US $ 2500, which will not fully compensate the Insured. Similarly if there is a depreciation clause of say 10% per year and if the accident happens after 2 years of purchase of the vehicle, then the depreciation is deducted from the claim amount apart from excess. The amount net of deductible and excess will be US $ 1,900. Two amounts have been deducted from US $ 3,000, an excess US $ 500 and depreciation US $ 600 (which is 20% of the cost of the door). In practice this principle may not be strictly applied in all types of policies but will act as a guide to the settlement of claims.

The following two Principles are supporting the Principle of Indemnity.

> Subrogation
> Contribution

d) Subrogation

It is one of the six principle, which supports the achievement of Indemnity. Suppose any third party is responsible for the damage to Insured car then the Insured has a right to claim from the party that was responsible for the damage to his car, moreover he can also claim from his Insurance Company. This gives the benefit of two claims to the Insured and he will definitely benefit from Insurance. In-order to avoid such a situation, where the Insured is in a better off position thereby violating the principle of Indemnity, the principal of Subrogation is applied, which helps in the achievement of the basic principle of Indemnity.

The Insurance Company applies the principle of Subrogation, which will help the Insurance Company recover the damages from the third party on behalf of their Insured. In laymen terms Subrogation is nothing but assuming the legal rights of a person for which the expenses or claim has been paid.

If Mr. A is driving his car on the road and Mr. B hits his car from behind as his brake failed at the last moment. Then Mr. A has a right to claim for the losses which he has incurred. Suppose the cost of repairing his car is US$ 1,000, then he has right to recover this amount from Mr. B. But if he has insurance then he has right to claim from his insurer. If he claims from Insurance Company and Mr. B then he will be in a better position and he is benefiting out of Insurance. Hence the Insurance Company will settle the claim and ask Mr. A to pay back the money he received from Mr. B. If Mr. B has not paid then the Insurance Company will ask Mr. A to provide a subrogation letter and will pursue the claim on behalf of A. Any amount recovered from B will go to the Insurance Company.

e) <u>Contribution</u>

This is another principle which is supporting the principle of Indemnity. In some cases there are chances that the Insured may buy more than one policy for the same risk.

This may happen due to various reasons, like the CEO may cover the same Vehicle as a part of his personal fleet and the Administration Manager may also cover the same Vehicle as a part of the Company Fleet. Some covers overlap and sometimes there may also be a deliberate attempt to commit fraud. If for one loss or claim, the insured approaches more than one Insurance Company and each company pays for the same loss then the Insured will be in a beneficial position. This situation is avoided by applying the principle of Indemnity. The Insurance Companies will not fully compensate the insured against the loss but they share the loss in the proportion of their liability.

For example if the CEO of a Company insures his car with XYZ Insurance Company as a part of his Householders Insurance Package and his Finance Manager includes the same car in the Company fleet policy with ABC Insurance Company then there is a duplication of insurance and if there is an accident to the car of the CEO and he incurs a loss of US$ 50,000. If he approaches both the Insurance Companies and he gets full settlement of his claim from both the Companies. Then the Insured will be in a better position by obtaining a compensation of US $ 100,000 against a loss of US $50,000. This will violate the principle of Indemnity.

In such situation principle of Contribution is applied. Assuming that the terms of both the Insurance Companies are similar then each Company will pay the loss in proportion. Company XYZ will pay an amount of US$ 25,000 and the Company ABC will pay the balance which is in equal proportion. This way the Insured is not benefitted from insurance. If both the Insurance Companies make full settlement of the claim then the Insured will be in a better position by obtaining a compensation of US $ 100,000 against a loss of US $50,000. This will violate the principle of Indemnity.

This way the insured will not get more than his loss. But by buying more than one policy he loses more premium, thus this principle will discourage the purchase of more than one policy by the insured and restrict the payment of claim so that the insured is not in a better position.

f) Proximate Cause

The last and tricky principle is known as the Proximate Cause. Normally it is difficult to pin point the cause of loss responsible for the loss or damage if there are more than one cause or overlapping causes. The Proximate cause can be the first cause or last cause or may be dominant cause. It is also defined as the cause which leads to a chain of events leading to the loss without the intervention of another event. If earthquake risk is excluded from the policy then if the fire is caused by the earthquake then the risk is excluded even though the damage is caused by the fire, which is covered in the policy.

Following of the two most quoted examples will clear the purpose and application of the principle of Proximate cause. A man purchases a Personal Accident Policy (which is an accidental death cover). In the first example he is riding a horse in a cold region and he falls from the horse. His leg is severely fractured and being a remote area, he is unable to find any help and due to severe cold he catches Pneumonia and dies. In the second example the person gets help and he is shifted to a hospital and he catches

Pneumonia. He dies due to Pneumonia. Here the Insurance Company has to decide as to which claim is payable. In both the cases there are two causes of death, accident and pneumonia, one is accidental and other one is due to a disease. The first case is treated as accidental and the claim is payable whereas the second case is treated as a death due to disease and the claim is not payable. However in case of death due to any cause both the cases would have been covered by the Insurance Policy.

There are risks which are insured and some are excluded. To identify whether a claim is payable or not we need to know the cause of loss. Once we know the cause of loss then we will be in a position to say that a particular loss is payable or not. Proximate cause helps us in identifying the root cause of loss in case of more than one cause or overlapping causes of loss. The identification helps us to find out whether cause of loss is coming under the insured peril, excluded peril or unnamed peril.

Other Legalities

- Independent Contract
- Cut Through Clause

- Independent Contract

Reinsurance is an independent contract and is

independent of the original insurance contract which is given to the Insured. The original contract is also termed as Insurance Policy and it is a guarantee that Insurer will pay the insured in case of loss due to an insured period up-to the sum agreed upon, irrespective of the Re-Insurance contract. In most of the cases the insured is not even aware of the presence of Reinsurance Contract. In case the Reinsurer goes bankrupt then the Insured has a right to claim from his Insurance Company. The Insurance Company cannot deny the claim of the insured for the reasons of the bankruptcies of the Reinsurers. If we look from the other side if the Insurance Company goes bankrupt then the Reinsurance recovery will not come to the Insured but it will go into the pool of the money kept for the creditors.

- ## Cut through Clause

Some Insured or Brokers may not be comfortable with the situation when the Insurance Company may become bankrupt. Hence to avoid the problems of such situation they may insist upon a clause which is known as "Cut through" clause. This allows the Reinsurers to pay to the insured directly in case the Insurance Company becomes bankrupt. It is very rarely asked for and very rarely granted by the Reinsurers.

As a general rule, we find most of the cases of disputes as far as the Re-insurance is concerned are settled out of court or through Arbitration. In case of escalation of dispute the domestic law of the Ceding or Insurance Company is applied.

4. <u>Benefits of Reinsurance</u>

Reinsurance provides numerous benefits to the Insurance Companies, Customers, Loss mitigating Organizations, Society and the Government. The following are some of the important benefits it provides to the Insurance Companies,

- Peace of Mind
- Increasing Underwriting Capacity
- Financial Stability
- Geographical Spread of Risk
- Solvency Margins and other Financial Features
- Providing Catastrophic Protection
- Risk Management and Underwriting Expertise
- Economic Development

- ## Peace of Mind

The first and foremost benefit of Reinsurance is that is gives peace of mind to the Insurer. The Insurance companies cede the risks to the Reinsurer in-order to save themselves from the major disasters. The cost of escaping from the loss and the quantum of loss is planned in advance. By paying a fixed amount of premium the Insurance Company is able to recover their major losses. They need not worry about the catastrophic losses, accumulation of losses, huge risks and capacities. Many good companies have made profits and paid bonuses to their employee's in-spite of bad years of losses because of robust Reinsurance program.

- ## Increasing Underwriting Capacity

When the Insurance Industry initially started few centuries ago the risks were fewer and simpler but as the complexities of the trade and industry increased and the growth of population led to increase in capacities of the factories. This led to the improvements of infrastructure and transportation. Now it is common to find movement of huge shipments in sea, air and road. This increase in the size of the risk will restrict the capacity of the Insurance Company to underwrite risks. In these types of scenario the Reinsurer will help underwriter to enhance their capacity. The Insurer will be able to write huge risks beyond their capacity with the support of Reinsurers.

A local Insurance Company has a capacity to write Property risk up-to US $10,000,000. If a factory wants to insure its risk for US $30,000,000 then the Insurance Company will be left with no option but to decline the risk in the absence of Reinsurance. Many a times Insurance Companies come across many tricky situation where it is not possible for the Insurance Companies to write the risks which are not in their treaty, are beyond the treaty limits or the risks are very unusual. In such situation Reinsurance comes to the rescue of the Insurance Companies and this will not only help the Insurance Companies to provide the cover but also to retain the risk.

- Financial Stability

A financial Stable organization is a boon to the society. As Insurance is a risky business, the results are usually fluctuating in the vibrant market. Broadly we say that the Underwriting result is Premium minus Claims. Due to bad year the result may be bad and due to good year the result may be good. If Tsunami had hit the coast in one year and Floods in the second year then the result may be bad for two years continuously. Large claims may also occur due to fire, terrorist attack or other acts of God. A single event may cause huge losses because of accumulation of the risk. Due to massive competition, the fluctuation may also occur due to various reasons like lack of application of law of large numbers like if a company is insuring a satellite and it become a failure.

The prime concern of Management of any Insurance Company is to see to it that the fluctuations in the underwriting results are eliminated. The stability of financial results will also help in greater confidence in the Insurance Company. There are many Insurance

Companies, who in-spite of their suffering major losses due to Catastrophes and Fires, which otherwise would have wiped out their companies are able to grow from strength to strength. This is mainly due to their prudent Reinsurance policies. Reinsurance will help in providing Financial Stability to the Insurance Company.

Some Insurance Companies have also become bankrupt due to lack of right reinsurance programs or due to non renewal of reinsurance programs.

- <u>Geographical Spread of Risk</u>

Another important benefit of Reinsurance is the Geographical Spread of the Risk. Risks emanating from Japan are spread throughout the world and any major loss in Japan is easily absorbed throughout the world by way of Reinsurance. The spread of the risk helps in achieving the concept of Law of large numbers. The Tsunami loss, twin tower attack Katrina losses were also absorbed throughout the world. However some companies were hit because of large retentions. But over-all it helped most of the Reinsurers in rewriting their strategies. The Reinsurers also should be aware of the accumulation of certain risks and they should see to it that the risk is properly spread by way of Co-reinsurance or Retrocession.

- <u>Solvency Margins and other Financial Features</u>

One of the requirements of a Regulator in the Regulated Markets is the requirement of maintaining the Solvency margin. If the Solvency margin is not maintained as required by the regulator then the regulator may impose harsh measures and may even lead to the cancellation of license. Apart from the regulatory aspect and also from business perspective a Company should have a good solvency margin. Reinsurance apart from providing financial stability to the Insurance Companies also helps them in maintaining good solvency ratios.

- Providing Catastrophic Protection

The Reinsurance arrangement helps in providing protection against accumulation of losses from catastrophic events. There may be catastrophic losses either from a single event causing huge losses or from an aggregation of many smaller claims arising out of single event. The Single event example can be taken as that of failure of launching of the satellite, a single event causing catastrophic loss to the Insurance Company. We can also take an example of aggregation of claims usually due to Floods or earthquake wherein many insured will be affected by the losses which ultimately will cause a huge loss to the Insurance Company.

- Risk Management and Underwriting Expertise

The Reinsurers have global presence and they have huge financial capacity along with long experience. This helps them understanding the risks better and they have a system of rating the risks and providing advices on the management of different Risks which otherwise the Insurance Companies may not have the capacity to understand. It also helps all the three involved getting into a synergistic relationship.

- **Economic Development**

The Reinsurance Companies require huge capital investments and they are custodians of huge funds provided by the Insurance Companies and this money is invested in the economy, which helps in economic development of the country and also helps in generating foreign exchange reserves to he country where the Reinsurers are based.

5. <u>Understanding Reinsurance</u>

We have defined the Reinsurance in during introduction. In simple terms it is insurance of insurance companies, protection purchased by Insurance companies or full or partial transfer of risk by the Insurance Companies.

<u>Types of Reinsurance</u>

There are two types of Reinsurance as follows,

- Proportional Reinsurance
- Non-proportional Reinsurance

- ## Proportional Reinsurance

Proportional reinsurance means reinsurers take an agreed or stated percent share of each policy that Insurance Company writes. In case of loss the Insurance Company and the Reinsurer share the losses in proportions agreed upon per the contract of Reinsurance. Whatever the Insurance Company receives in premium will be passed on to the Reinsurer in the agreed percentage and the claims are also settled in the same proportion.

The Insurance Company receives Ceding commission to cover the cost of procurement and servicing of the business mainly Administration expenses, procurement commission, marketing expenses and other relevant expenses. If we look minutely the Premium, Risk and the Losses are shared in agreed proportion or percentage basis.

Let us have a look at the following example, by virtue of financial capacity or regulation the ABC Insurance Company may be allowed to write a business of US $10,000,000. But by Reinsuring the Insurance Company may be in a position to write a business of more than US$10,000,000. In order to write a higher amount of business some Insurance Companies also insure a larger risk with more than one Reinsurer.

Proportional Reinsurance is usually done under the following heads,

- ➤ Facultative

- ➤ Facultative Obligatory

- ➤ Quota Share Treaty

- ➤ Surplus Treaty,

- ➤ Open Cover and Pools

Before we proceed further let us examine an example of **surplus Reinsurance** or surplus line of treaty. In such cases, a retained "line" is defined as retention - say US $10,000,000. In a 4 line surplus treaty the *reinsurer* accepts up-to US $40,000,000, which come to 4 lines. If the insurance company issues a policy for $8,000,000, they would keep all risk, premiums and losses from that policy. If they issue a $20,000,000 policy, they would share half of the premiums and losses with the *reinsurer* (1 line each). The maximum underwriting capacity of the Insurance Company would be $ 10,000,000 in this example.

Non-proportional Reinsurance

In recent years we find more use of non-proportional Reinsurance. It is considered to be economical and effective way of controlling losses. In late 19th century it emerged as an alternative form of Reinsurance compared to the proportional form of Reinsurance. In Non-proportional Reinsurance the premiums and Loss (claims are not shared in proportion). Usually in these type of contracts the liability between the Insurance Company and the Reinsurer is focused on the basis of Loss occurring. In the earlier example we have seen that the premiums and claims were proportionate, even the risk sharing is proportionate. But whereas in this case the risk is shared on the basis of loss occurring. In non-proportional Reinsurance the losses up-to a limit is borne by the Insurance Company and the balance is transferred to the Reinsurers up-to an agreed amount. The Reinsurers would like to safeguard their losses and may like to cap their losses by applying an upper limit to the losses.

Suppose there is a huge loss then the Insurance Company may bear a certain amount of loss after that the loss is transferred to the Reinsurer up-to a certain limit. The loss and the premium are not correlated. However the premium is usually based on the proportion of premiums received on a particular risk or turnover of the Insurance Company.

Non-Proportional Reinsurance is divided into following types,

> ➢ Excess of Loss
> ➢ Stop Loss

If an Insurance Company purchases an Excess of Loss Insurance over US$ 25,000,000 and with a limit of US$ 100,000,000. In case of loss of US$ 50,000,000, the Insurance Company will bear the loss of US$25,000,000 and the Reinsurance Company will bear the loss of US$ 25,000,000. In the same example if the loss is US $ 125,000,000 then the Insurance Company will pay US $25,000,000 and Re-insurer will pay US $ 100,000,000. If the loss exceeds then the losses will ball back to the Insurance Company. It will be the responsibility of the Insurance Company to have further Re-insurance if necessary. The concept of stop loss is explained in the last part.

Forms of Reinsurance

There are two basic forms of Reinsurance as below,

- Facultative Reinsurance
- Treaty Reinsurance

- <u>Facultative Reinsurance</u>

Facultative Reinsurance is also known as case by case Insurance or Optional Insurance.

It is the oldest form of Reinsurance. In this type of the Reinsurance the Reinsurers have an option to accept or decline risks which are offered to them, even the insurer also have a right to place or not to place a risk.

It is done on an individual risk basis, depending upon the protection needs, the Insurance Companies request for coverage from Reinsurers. They have to provide full details of the risk being offered to the Reinsurance Company. The details are provided in a format usually known as Slip. Equipped with the information in the slip and additional reports, the Insurance Companies approach different Reinsurers and the Reinsurers evaluate each request and take a decision regarding acceptance or rejection of the risk. It is the prerogative of the Reinsurers to accept or decline a particular risk.

It is used as a complementary insurance to the Obligatory or Treaty Reinsurance. It is mostly placed on a proportional basis. The cover starts with the acceptance of the Insurance by the Insurance Company and ends with the expiry of the Policy.

As we know that renewal is treated as a new contract. At the time of renewal the Insurers have to follow the procedure offer and acceptance of the risk means they have to provide all the details of the risk including any changes to the policy and other terms and the Reinsurer again have a right either to continue with the cover or decline the offer.

Advantages of Facultative Insurance to the Insurers or Cedants.

One of the major Advantages to the Insurance Company is that it provides with a flexibility to arrange Reinsurance. In case the Insurance Company is comfortable with the risk they can retain the risk with themselves and need not go to the Reinsurer.

It helps in taking up the businesses of its customers, which otherwise would have been declined. It enhances its business relationship with the customers and helps in retaining the existing business and getting new business.

The Insurance Company is free from the responsibility of reciprocal business.

It provides stability to its Underwriting results as bad risk or big risks are transferred to the Reinsurer.

Since Facultative Reinsurance is an individual contracts the bad performance of the contract will not have any adverse impact to the Insurance Company and it has option to go for another Reinsurer.

Facultative Insurance also helps the Insurers in getting the terms of Specialist Insurances. As the Insurers do not have the expertise to rate or provide with the quotation to some types of Risks.

As the International Reinsurance market is wide and varied. It helps them in placing any kind of Risk with the right Reinsurer.

Disadvantages of Facultative Insurance

One of the major draw-backs of the Facultative Reinsurance is that it is expensive as each risk has to be worked out individually and the cost of administering it goes up, depending upon the type of risk.

The Insurer cannot confirm cover until he gets the confirmation from one of the Reinsurers. It places the Insurers in a bad situation. Especially if the customer is having a close renewal date or policy has expired. The Insurance Company has to make adequate precautions not to confirm the cover until the Reinsurers accept their proposal and terms.

Facultative Insurance is risk and bit difficult to operate compared to Treaty operations. There are circumstances when even more than 40 Reinsurers have declined the risk after getting information upon information.

The Insurer may be faced with difficult situation with the Reinsurers, if they demand higher rates and higher

deductible, which may not be acceptable to the local Market. They may even demand implementation of Claims Cooperation Clause.
Any change to the Policy has to be agreed upon by the Reinsurer, which again puts the onus upon the Insurers.

If the Insurance by oversight is unable to inform the Reinsurer about the renewal of the policy and if any loss occurs the liability will be to the Insurance Company Account.

Facultative Reinsurance is usually done in the following circumstances,

❖ When the treaty is full
❖ When the risk is outside the scope of the treaty
❖ If the risk is unusual

• <u>Treaty Reinsurance</u>

Treaty Insurance is also known as Obligatory Reinsurance and Automatic Insurance. Under Treaty Reinsurance the Reinsurer is obliged to accept cessions within the terms and conditions of the agreement and the Insurer are obliged to cede the Risk. Under treaty the reinsurer cannot refuse to accept the risk which are within the scope of the agreement, however they have every right to deny any risk which is outside the scope of the treaty. The Reinsurance started with the Facultative Insurance but Treaty became a more popular form of Insurance.

Whole portfolios of risks which are similar are covered under the treaty insurance. Both the Insurer and the

Reinsurer are obliged to cede and accept the risks respectively on terms agreed upon.

This type of Reinsurance is done both on proportional and non-proportional basis. Under proportional basis, the risks are shared in agreed proportion. Treaty is an annual contract with continuation and is subject to cancellation clause. The contract can also be long term like 4 year or 5 year. Some life contracts duration can last up-to 30 years.

Quota Share Treaty

Under Quota Share Treaty a fixed proportion of risk is retained by the Insurance Company or the Ceding Company, the portion may be belonging to particular class or it may belong to the entire business written by the Insurance Company and the rest is transferred to the Re-insurer in the agreed proportion.

The following example will help us in understanding the concept of Quota Share Treaty.

An XYZ Insurance Company takes a decision to take a Re-insurance program on Quota share basis. Based on the market conditions and its capacity it may decide to retain a certain percentage of the risks on one or all major classes of businesses like Fire. The risk is shared on pro-rata basis in particular or all classes of business the premium and claims are shared in similar proportions.

If XYZ put its Fire portfolio to Quota Share Treaty in the ratio of 20: 80 percent the upper limit of US$10,000,000. The Insurance Company accepts a risk of manufacturing unit against Fire risk with a sum insured of US $1000,000/-. The Insurance Company will retain US $ 200,000 and the balance is placed with the Reinsurer. Any amount above the cap limit will fall back to the Insurance Company and they need to make other arrangements for covering or retaining such risk. The percentage and the caps may differ on different treaties. Here the risk, premium and claims are shared on proportionate basis. The Insurance Company will get the Commission for placing the business with the Reinsurer.

Advantages of Quota Share Treaty

This is a good scheme for the Insurance Companies which has started their business. This is also good for Companies which lack experience in particular class of business or where the risks are bigger.

It also helps in restricting the losses.

This type of Insurance is also helpful in reducing the Administrative costs.

It helps in removing the un-certainty of securing coverage.

This method of Reinsurance is better for both the Re-insurance Company and the Insurance Company.

The new Insurance Companies have a flexibility of scaling up the proportion of share of business in case of good experience and scaling down the proportion of share of business in case of bad experience.

Disadvantages of Quota Share Treaty

All the risks in a particular type or all similar types of risk passes on to the Reinsurance Company, the benefits also passes on to the Re-insurers. The Insurance Company has no choice but to share good and bad risks in the proportion agreed upon. If the Insurance Company portfolio is profitable then the benefit of profit goes to the Reinsurer.

The scheme lacks flexibility as we find in other types of Reinsurance programs.

Surplus Treaty

In this type of Reinsurance program, the Insurance Company or the Ceding Company will try to evaluate its retention program in one or more class or all classes of Risks. Once it understands and fixes its retention limits then it can go for Surplus Reinsurance.

The Insurance Company exposure is limited to amount of risk it is willing to take. It helps the Insurance Company to accept large risks and making its upper loss limit similar in-spite of larger risks in its portfolio.

Here the insurance is done on the basis of lines. The Insurance Company can retain one or more lines of for retention and the balance lines it can place with one or more Reinsurance Companies. The Insurance Company will decide about its retention limit and then places the balance amount with the Reinsurer up-to a certain limit and if the limit is crossed then the balance will fall back to the Insurance Company unless they have other Reinsurance program. ABC Insurance Company has a Surplus treaty with a Reinsurance Company the retention is one line of US $ 10,000,000 and the Reinsurer has a 9 lines limitation. Any risk below 10,000,000 will be retained by the Insurance Company, whereas any risk above 10,000,000 will be passed on to the Reinsurer up-to the 9 line limit. In case of transfer the losses are also shared in proportion. The risks which are above the retention limit of the Insurance Company will make them share it as per the agreement and the proportion agreed upon. The risk, premiums and claims are shared in the agreed proportion.

The following example with a line of US $ 10,000,000 and a cap of 9 lines, will help us in understanding the concept in right perspective, if the sum insured for a Fire Risk is US $ 5,000,000 then the Insurance Company will retain the risk and it will not go to the Surplus treaty, whereas if a Fire Risk is US $ 50,000,000. Then the Insurance Company will retain US$10,000,000 and the balance which is US $40,000,000 will be passed on to the Surplus treaty Reinsurer. If the gross premium received is US$5,000 then the premium retained by the Insurance Company will be US$1,000 and the Reinsurer will receive an amount of US $ 4,000. In case of claim of US$50,000 the Insurance Company will pay US$ 10,000 and the Reinsurer will pay US $ 40,000.

There can be a single surplus treaty or some time it may be more than one Surplus treaty known as First Surplus Treaty and Second Surplus Treaty etc.

In majority of cases Fire Insurances the liability per original risk is not defined in terms of sum Insured but is usually defined in terms of Estimated Maximum Loss (EML, PML, MPL).

In case of Liability and Accident classes it may be the amount of Indemnity.

The Insurance can go in for a combination of Quota Share Treaty as well as Surplus Treaty together, depending upon the requirements and convenience.

Facultative Obligatory

Facultative Obligatory cover is an arrangement which has the benefits of Facultative cover and Surplus Treaty cover. In this the Insurance Company has an option not to automatically cede the risks to the Reinsurers. But the Reinsurer has to accept all the cessions within the limits agreed upon subject to the retention by the Insurance Company. Usually the commission is low in this type of arrangement but it is definitely beneficial to the Insurance Companies. It is usually used to cover the risks which are of irregular nature and of high exposure.

Open Covers - They are seen more as a type of Facultative cover rather than a treaty cover. Here the Insurance Company can place the business of certain commodities without any restriction as to its retention and up-to the limits agreed upon by the Reinsurer.

Pools - In this type of Reinsurance, it is like a joint

underwriting operation. In this the Insurance and the Reinsurance companies form a collective capacity or pool in one or more classes of business and it is retro-ceded to the members as agreed upon in proportion. This is more useful in catastrophic exposures.

Excess of Loss

Excess of loss is a kind of non-proportional Reinsurance where the Insurance Company agrees to absorb an amount of loss occurring due to one event in a particular class or all classes of business and then it transfers the balance to the Reinsurance Company. It can be arranged based on per risk basis or per event basis. Let us take the example of Tsunami, which occurred and caused a devastating loss of life and property. XYZ Insurance Company had an excess of loss cover per event risk with retention of US$ 1,000,000 and it suffers a loss of US $ 5,000,000 in losses due to Tsunami and the cause of loss is identified to a peril insured against. Then the Insurance Company will retain the loss of US$1,000,000 to its account and the balance amount of US$ 4,000,000 will be paid by the Reinsurers. But if the loss is less then US$1,000,000 then the claim will be fully paid by the XYX Insurance Company.

Advantages of Excess of Loss covers

The Insured Company is protected against huge exposures, in the absence of this cover the Company may wind up due to huge losses.

Administrative costs are lower for both the Insurance Company and the Reinsurer.

For the Reinsurer the exposure is less as most of the small claims are retained by the Insurance Company and handled by them without the involvement of the Reinsurer.

Disadvantages of Excess of Loss covers

In case of real bad loss experience the Insurance Company will end up paying more premiums to overcome the loss ratio.

The calculation of premium may prove to be bit difficult as there is no relationship between the premium charged to the Insured and the premium charged by the Reinsurance Company.

In case of reinstatement provision the Insurance Company may end up paying the premium more than once depending upon the number of losses in a year.

In case of small losses the Insurance Company ends up paying all the losses without availing the benefit of Reinsurance.

Stop Loss Cover

Another type of non-proportional Reinsurance is known as Stop Loss Cover. If there is an increase in the claims frequency, the Insurance Company may find it-selves in difficult condition and may ultimately end up making losses and their loss ratios may get aggravated. To help Insurance Companies avoid such situations Stop Loss cover is available. In Stop Loss cover the loss ratio of the

Insurance Company is stopped at a certain percentage which is agreed upon by both the Insurance and Reinsurance Companies. If the loss in any one calendar year exceeds the loss ratio agreed upon the Reinsurer's will pay the remaining claim up-to an upper cap limit. This is usually a privileged cover provided to reliable Insurance companies.

Let us have a look into the following example, if an Insurance company purchases a stop loss cover of 110% of amount in excess of 80% loss ratio. In this case the loss of up-to 80% will be borne by the Insurance Company but if the loss ratio crosses 80% then the losses over and above 80% is paid by the Reinsurer and up-to a limit of 110%. Any losses above 110% will fall back on the Insurance Company.

6. Designing Re-Insurance Programme

Identify and Analyze the basics for Reinsurance

Before getting into any Reinsurance arrangement, it is better both the parties to the Re-insurance contract have a proper understanding of the arrangement of the Risk Transfer. The insurer should understand the exact form of reinsurance required and other parameters like retention, coverage and the limits of Reinsurance required.

The Insurers and the Re-insurers must have the following objectives before they can enter into any sort of agreement,

- To know the class or classes of Insurance's being involved.

- To understand the geographical distribution of the risks, and whether there is any accumulation of the risks.
- Past loss experiences during various period and due to various events.
- To know the exposed values of the large risks and the loss mitigation programs.
- Who are the customers of the Insurance Company.
- The management record of both the Companies.
- To be fully be aware of the Regulatory environment and the attitudes of the society at large.
- To see to it that the compliance of the Insurance regulatory requirements are not violated due to the Reinsurance program.
- The currency fluctuations, especially if the Re-insurers are located in a different country. This may increase the cost of Insurance due to currency fluctuations.
- To analyze the social and economic conditions of the country as this will have an impact on the achievement of the agreement between the Insurers and the Reinsurer.
- To Re-insurer and Insurer should know the cost of procurement and manageability of the portfolios.
- The Insurance Company should know whether the Reinsurers have strong Retrocession treaties with reliable Reinsurers.

The Insurance Company should be able to analyze and identify the exposures to its portfolios by the size and type of risks. The exposure can be EML in property insurance, limit of liability and legal expenses in liability insurance and sum insured in most of the other Classes. Once it identifies the exposures then it can fix its retentions. Retentions are decided based on many factors. The main purpose to have an underwriting stability, as a custodian of funds belonging to the insured the Insurance Company should see to it that the money is adequately protected. The other parameter which effects retention is the regulation, which may prescribe minimum level of retentions the Insurance Companies. After technical and financial analysis of the portfolios is done on individual class basis and on combined portfolio basis the company will be in a position to decide about the retention levels.

However the final decision vests with the management of the Companies as they play a major role in deciding as to the right levels of retention in each class of business and for the over-all Company. Their decisions are based on the Corporate Strategy. Retention should always be based upon the loss ratio, the probability of loss and profitability.

Selecting the right Reinsurance Programme

Once the retention levels are decided then the Insurance Company has to select the right type of Reinsurance Program and the right Reinsurers.

We have seen various types of Reinsurance Programs earlier in the book. The Insurance companies based upon their financial analysis and technical analysis will be in a position to take a decision as to the suitable type of reinsurance. In case of non-proportional reinsurance it will help in protecting the Insurance Companies from loss only after a certain limit. In case of proportional reinsurance the losses are shared for each and every claim and this will reduce the portion of liability of the Insurer.

The Facultative reinsurance which is optional reinsurance is found to be costly, time consuming and uncertain. Due to which most of the insurances are on the basis of Treaty. After having a treaty also Insurers can also use Facultative form of reinsurance depending on the need and requirement.

If we analyze the Quota share treaty we find that it will help in reducing the cost of claims. In case of Surplus treaty, the claims beyond a certain limit are transferred if the risk is ceded to the reinsurers and if the risk is not ceded to the reinsurer then the losses are to the Insurance Company. If we analyze Excess of loss treaty, we find that this type of reinsurance will be helpful in providing coverage for large risks. Stop loss is good for Companies which are new to the business or writing a certain class of business.

The Insurance Company is free to choose one or more type of Reinsurers or treaties to have an optimal level of coverage to its portfolio. Some of the factors need to be considered before getting into a type of treaty are as follows,

- Regulatory requirement
- Cost of procurement
- Management of the operations
- Purpose of Reinsurance program
- Reciprocal exchange
- Handling costs
- Retention capacity

Placement of the Reinsurance Program

After identifying and analyzing the Reinsurance requirements and Selection of Reinsurance program the next step is the placement o the Reinsurance Program. The Insurance Company has to decide in which market it is better to place the risk and whether it should be either direct or through a broker. In some markets a broker has to be involved for placement whereas in some markets direct placement can be done. A vast majority of Reinsurers are from the countries which has a strong regulatory control and these companies are financially very sound and a very high rating.

Hence placing directly business with these companies is not only secure but also prestigious. It again depends upon the Insurance Company which is placing the business if the Insurance Company is reputed then it will not be difficult for it to find a good Re-insurer. But if the Insurance Company is a new company, then it will be easier for it to approach a broker to get the right coverage. In-case of risks with large capacities also we need to seek the services of the brokers. Broker by virtue of their experience, market knowledge and relationship with the Reinsurers will be able to place the business in the international market. He will also be in a position to administer the business to the satisfaction of both the Insurers and the Reinsurer.

The Insurance Company should be able to provide right information and get the right rates, apart from rate they should also see to it that the commission structure is negotiated in such a way as to get an optimal benefit to both.

Reviewing the Reinsurance Program

The best Reinsurance Program also has to be reviewed as we are living in a dynamic environment. Each day changes are occurring, which are in the form of new risks, currency fluctuations, wars, economic recession, bankruptcies, Tsunami, etc., The Review should be a continuous process and it should begin well ahead of time. At the time of review the following, need to be thoroughly analyzed.

- Services of the Reinsurers including Claims processing and settlement
- Financial Rating of the Reinsurers
- Cost of Reinsurance
- Commission structure
- Current Underwriting policy of the Insurance Company
- Financial requirements
- Technical Requirements

- Countries of operation of the Reinsurer
- Reinsurer's Regulatory changes
- Impact of currency of the Reinsurer
- Insurers Regulatory Requirement

Insurance Companies should have a good and robust review system. This will help in providing adequate security at a reasonable cost. Unfortunately most of the Reinsurance Reviews are done only before the renewal of the treaties. Due to paucity of time the reviews are not done properly and the Insurance Companies end up renewing the treaties with the same terms and conditions, which otherwise would have yielded a good savings if proper review had been done at the right time.

7. **Reinsurance Glossary**

Bordereau - Form providing premium or Claim data with respect to identified risks which is furnished the reinsurer by the reinsured.

Capacity - The amount (value) of *exposure* that an insurer or *reinsurer* is willing to place at risk. Capacity may be applied to a single risk, a program, a line of business, or an entire book of business.

Cede - When an Insurance company reinsures its liability with another, the term "cede" is used.

Ceding Commission - The *cedant's acquisition costs* and overhead expenses, taxes, other fees, plus a fee representing a share of expected profits.

Ceding Company - The original or primary insurer, the Insurance company which purchases reinsurance.

Commission - The reinsurer allows the Insurance company a ceding or direct commission allowance on gross premiums received from them, the purpose is to cover the procurement expenses of the Insurance Company.

Errors and Omissions Clause – It is similar to the one used in insurance. It is a provision in reinsurance agreement, which is intended to make ineffective any change in liability or benefits as a result of an inadvertent error by either party.

Ex Gratia Payment – It is a payment made for which the Reinsurers are not liable under the terms of its policy. This type of payment is very rarely used by the Re-insurer.

Experience: Statistical expression of events connected with insurance, of outgo/loss, or of income, actual or estimated.

Following the Fortunes - The clause stipulates that once a risk has been ceded by the reinsured, the reinsurer is bound by the same fate thereon as experienced by the ceding company.

Incurred Loss Ratio - The percentage of losses incurred to premiums earned.

Intermediary – An Intermediary is a third party who is involved in the process of procuring the reinsurance contract agreement. They are the experts in their field and they recommend the insurance companies as to the best cover, terms and reinsurers available in the market.

Lead Reinsurer - The *reinsurer* who negotiates the terms, conditions, and premium *rates* and usually first to sign is termed as Lead Reinsurer.

Loss Event - Loss even is an event causing losses to the ceding company or to the reinsurer resulting from a single cause such as a Tsunami.

Loss Ratio – It is a relationship between the incurred losses to earned premiums expressed as a percentage.

Peril - Peril refers to the cause of possible loss. For example in the property insurance, we consider Fire, Windstorm, Collision, Hail, etc as perils.

Per Risk Excess Reinsurance - Retention and amount of reinsurance applied on "per risk" basis.

Deposit Premium – It is the advance premium collected in lump-sum, when the computation of final premium cannot be done in advance. This premium is treated like a deposit premium is necessary adjustments are made as and when the final premium is arrived at.

Reinstatement Value Clause – On occurrence of a loss, the reinsurance coverage under the treaty is reduced after payment of loss against that coverage. The reinsurance provides automatic cover on payment of necessary reinstatement premium.

Retention - The net amount of risk which the ceding company or the reinsurer keeps for its own account.

Retrocession - In simple terms it is nothing but reinsurance of reinsurance.

Risks - A term used to denote the physical units of property at risk or the object of insurance protection. Sometime is it used to refer to perils and/or hazard. The correct definition of Risk is "uncertainty of loss occurring"

Slip – It is also known as binder. It is a cover note often including more than one reinsurer. At Lloyd's of London, the slip is carried from underwriter to underwriter for initialing and subscribing to a specific share of the risk.

8. <u>Twenty Major Re-insurers</u>

Twenty Major International Re-insurers are as follows,

1. Munich Reinsurance Company

2. Swiss Reinsurance Company Limited

3. Hannover Rueckversicherung AG

4. Berkshire Hathaway Inc.

5. Lloyd's

6. SCOR S.E.

7. Reinsurance Group of America Inc.

8. Allianz S.E.

9. PartnerRe Ltd.

10. Everest Re Group Ltd.

11. Transatlantic Holdings Inc.

12. Korean Reinsurance Company

13. China Reinsurance (Group) Corporation

14. London Reinsurance Group Inc.

15. MAPFRE RE, Compania de Reaseguros, S.A.

16. General Insurance Corporation of India

17. Assicurazioni Generali SpA

18. AEGON N.V.

19. QBE Insurance Group Limited

20. XL Group plc

ABOUT THE AUTHOR

Mohammed Sadullah Khan, Faculty Member, Chartered Insurance Practitioner, Insurance Studies Unit, The Institute of Banking (Saudi Arabian Monetary Agency), an MBA (University topper), is a Fellow of Insurance Institute of India and a Fellow of Chartered Insurance Institute (UK). Has more than 25 years of experience in the Insurance Industry, of which 18 years in Saudi Arabia. Was Insurance Columnist for one of the leading English Daily, has written numerous articles.

He can be reached at mosakhan40@gmail.com. www.generalawarenessforall.blogspot.com